MOVEME

MOVEME

Harnessing the Power of Your Thoughts for Personal & Professional Greatness

Marcal Graham, Ed.D

In collaboration with
Leadership Builders, Inc.

iUniverse, Inc.
New York Bloomington

MOVEME
Harnessing the Power of Your Thoughts for Personal and Professional Greatness

iUniverse books may be ordered through booksellers or by contacting:

iUniverse
1663 Liberty Drive
Bloomington, IN 47403
www.iuniverse.com
1-800-Authors (1-800-288-4677)

Because of the dynamic nature of the Internet, any Web addresses or links contained in this book may have changed since publication and may no longer be valid.

ISBN: 978-1-4502-3512-9 (sc)
ISBN: 978-1-4502-3514-3 (dj)
ISBN: 978-1-4502-3513-6 (ebk)

Printed in the United States of America

iUniverse rev. date: 8/11/2010

This book is dedicated to so many, but I must start with God first and foremost.

To my family of Marion and Charjuan Graham, who read countless rewrites and encouraged me to dig deep inside of myself and my expereinces. I look forward to reading your book!

To Renee Hemsley, who edited revisions and offered much food for thought. Thank you for your feedback and strength on this book.

To my Charlotte Team: Wendi Smith, director of Match Support, and Julie Moore, director of Enrollment at Big Brothers & Sisters of Charlotte. Thank you for pushing me to start this book and for providing an opportunity to put my thoughts into practice with your two teams. Thank you for the love and lunches!

Elijah Watson, you are my best supporter in Charlotte. Thank you for your brotherly support and for encouraging others to take note of my books.

Wanda Jones, thank you for being a great sounding board and a great person. I wish you continued success as you prepare to do your own thing.

Shelton Jeffries, principal of West Charlotte High. Thank you for your wisdom, determination, and intelligence.

Acknowledgments

Rev. Johnnie Wallace, I thank you for being the first to expose students in Charlotte collectively to my first book on leadership. Thank you for the kind words of inspiration.

Reginald Johnson and family, I look forward to us working together. Thanks for the inspirational conversations by phone on our way to work.

I would like to thank the Magic Johnson Foundation and the Youth Leadership Foundation for their support.

To those students and adults who read my books, I hope reading my work has helped you in your life. Every day is a challenge!

CONTENTS

PREFACE

I define *reflection* as the process of uncovering the real or true self. It is my belief that the thoughts and reflections of people cannot be summed up in one book. Therefore, this is the first book in a series to address reshaping people's mind-set. This leadership and reflection series is for individuals who want to grow intellectually, professionally, and personally. We plant a seed, then water and nurture it so that it becomes strong and healthy. This should be the same model for our mind-set. For those who want to grow, be challenged, believe in being open-minded, and are self-motivated, this is the first step toward channeling your potential into action. Through this series, I am looking to change people's thinking and ultimately their behavior so that they have a better chance of becoming the person they aspire to be—or in the words of Gretchen Rubin in *The Happiness Project,* "identify the concrete actions that will boost your happiness."[1]

THE KEY TO REFLECTION: THE MOVEME PROCESS

MOVEME is not a job; it is a process for rethinking who you are as a person. Personal success is determined more than by dollars and cents. Several core personal qualities separate those who value short-lived happiness over long-term success. The acronym of MOVEME stands for these six ideas:

---

1   Gretchen Rubin, *The Happiness Project* (New York: HarperCollins Publishers, 2009), p. xiii.

Motivation
Openness
Vision
Exposure
Mastery
Engagement

Motivation is a term that many people are familiar with and practice daily. The question is to what degree individuals are motivated to do things that take them out of their comfort zone in order to strive for excellence. How often do you step up to personal and professional challenges that require you to generate a high level of motivation even in the face of adversity? It is easy to be motivated with things that you enjoy, but do you motivate yourself to overcome professional obstacles with colleagues and supervisors in the workplace? How do you generate positive energy to overcome these challenges?

Openness is not as common a mind-set as you might believe. Unfortunately, there are individuals who are unwilling to change their way of thinking or even listen to new ideas that may be beneficial to their growth, personally and professionally. When you practice openness, you are leaving open the possibility that you may be wrong, misguided, or misinformed about a person, situation, or event. You allow room to make decisions rationally and with much thought. How do you react when people disagree with you? Do you block thoughts that may put your thinking in a vulnerable place? Being vulnerable positions your mind to grow and confront new ideas.

Vision deals with the ability to see beyond the surface of situations. Many individuals, because of their limited experiences or exposure, lack the ability to see beyond what is directly in front of them. They have not planned or prepared for success, so when adversity appears they are unable to adapt or reinvent their thinking in order to accomplish their goal. There is one potential downside to being a "forward thinker," and that's only seeing the big picture and not the smaller challenges and victories along the way.

Exposure is a critical part of the MOVEME mind-set because it encourages you to think about the kinds of experiences you have been exposed to in your life, whether through family, friends, education, or work. The decisions that you make are, to a large part, based on the experiences you have had throughout your life, so you must understand both the positive aspect and the limitations to this thinking. We must be conscious about the types of movies, hobbies, people, and things that we read and do daily. The best scenario would be to have a healthy balance of experiences to pull from, but who determines what is healthy and what is not? How do you know when your exposure to people is limited? Can this be changed? Is it simply sitting down and talking to people of different cultures and backgrounds?

Mastery is by far the easiest to understand since it poses two questions to you. Have you dedicated yourself to excellence in everything that you do in life? Are you reaching down within your emotional, physical, and mental self to work on things in your life that you have control over?

Engagement is critical to your success. To get things accomplished, you may be required to interact with groups, organizations, and the community at large. You are not an island, so you must develop strategies, interventions, and approaches that promote your personal and professional success. Through engagement, you are trying to reach people and make connections from "real relationships" with people who may not see the value in self-reflection.

These are all abstract terms that drive us to be something or someone. They are measured in action and results. We want to uncover the thoughts behind the actions and develop ideas that help to move your thinking.

The mission of the MOVEME process is to create safe neighborhoods and healthy families, educate them, and help build a productive workforce.

THE THINKING AND DRIVING FORCE BEHIND MOVEME

MOVEME bridges thoughts to action and provides connectedness. We are trying to cross racial, class, and generational boundaries in order to have an effective and long-term relationship with one another. We want to plant seeds of self-motivation, personal resiliency, and reflection. One of the objectives is to address underlying issues that may undermine personal growth and leadership development. Therefore, understanding and developing strategies for addressing how individuals deal with personal, financial, and professional adversity and make choices is a constant undertaking. Instilling in people strategies for dealing with challenging situations is an important and ongoing goal of this process.

While I do not claim to have all the answers, I have spent considerable time researching leadership within schools and communities and talking with students, parents, teachers, principals, and administrators. I grew up in a single-parent home, guided by my mother, which provided a great foundation for the man I am today. Even having a great mother, I had to be resolute and intentional about what I wanted out of life at an early age. Rather than always learning through the school of hard knocks, I listened a great deal to mentors and role models. I realized that by reflecting and observing I could increase my likelihood of success.

The roots of the MOVEME Group are in understanding what motivates youth. During the last year of my doctoral work (2003–2004), I had the honor to work with the Bill Cosby Academic Posse Program at Temple University. Through this program I was able to work with middle school students who were highly motivated and engaged in improving their writing, math, and science abilities. The students were taught and tutored by master retired and current teachers from the School District of Philadelphia. Certainly the academic help was an integral part of the program. In addition, the exposure students gained from art galleries, cultural dance performances, basketball games, and trips to New York City helped to move their mind-set, encouraging them to reflect on their own communities and the possibilities that they could realize if they applied themselves daily to excellence.

On a sunny Saturday in October 2007, I had the opportunity to speak to high school students at Howard University in Washington DC about leadership. I presented the MOVEME principles to students and parents mostly from Prince George's County and Washington DC. It was amazing to hear students express how inspirational and motivational MOVEME was to them over the hour presentation. Not only were students attentive and asked questions, but they started to really reflect on how they needed to become leaders in their personal and academic lives. It was the first time I had let MOVEME out for public consumption, and their feedback was invaluable. Although I was presenting to small groups of students, it still provided me with the impetus for understanding the power of leadership. Even parents offered positive feedback and expressed how they needed to display greater leadership and personal responsibility over their own lives.

THEORETICAL UNDERPINNINGS

I am an avid reader, so while I was in Cambridge, Massachusetts, I visited a bookstore and came across a book that helped me put MOVEME into a relevant context. It was by accident that I picked up *Leadership on the Line*, by Ronald Heifetz and Marty Linsky.[2] In their discussion of leadership they state,

---

2   Ronald Heifetz & Marty Linsky, *Leadership on the Line* (Boston: Harvard Business School, 2002), p. 2.

> To lead is to live dangerously because when leadership counts, when you lead people through difficult change, you challenge what people hold dear—their daily habits, tools, loyalties, and ways of thinking—with nothing more than a possibility. Moreover, leadership often means exceeding the authority you are given to tackle the challenge at hand. People push back when you disturb the personal and institutional equilibrium they know.

In addition to this passage, the authors highlight what MOVEME is trying to address in people: adaptive pressures that we all face in our personal and professional lives. According to Heifetz and Linsky, these adaptive challenges are not solved by having expert or technical knowledge, but rather require unorthodox approaches, new discoveries, changing attitudes, values, and behaviors, which must be internalized if true leadership is to take shape. More specifically, we must see evidence that a person has actually overcome obstacles as a result of changing his thinking or attitude. In order for individuals to engage in this process they must be willing to undergo a transformation, just as coal must be transformed in order to become a diamond. Heifetz and Linsky remind us that individuals cannot postpone the adaptive process or avoid it if they are to overcome obstacles that stand in the way of them becoming a leader.

USING THIS BOOK

The workbook format of this book is essential if we are to identify and dismantle the mind-sets and attitudes that we harbor as result of learned and accepted behaviors. This leadership and reflection series is a challenge to those of us who want to take charge over the "little things" in life: our time, life, and happiness. The questions posed to you are meant to encourage you to think deeply and develop ownership in this process of self-exploration. There are no ready-made answers, but a challenge to the person who wants to engage in this process. You must be willing to think, reflect, rethink, and hopefully make changes that are life-altering. This book is a living document that is intended to capture the thoughts, feelings, and actions that undermine and promote personal and professional growth.

Each chapter has a short introduction, followed by engaging questions that "assess your state of mind" and concluding thoughts.

THE CONCEPT OF MOVEME

My vision for MOVEME was shaped by my upbringing and experiences as a youth. My mother, who raised me by herself, was my main role model. Her work ethic, nurturing ways, and tenacity helped to build my foundation and high level of expectations that I set for myself. My mother's influence, which provided strength and direction, and her emphasis on faith, leadership, ethics, and academic excellence provided structure in my life.

Through observation and practice, I learned responsibility and accountability at a young age. While my mother worked, she relied on me to prepare meals, clean, and supervise and ensure the safety of my sister. In addition, I had to maintain at least a B average academically. I realized that in order to achieve anything in life, I must be highly motivated. Often, I generated my own positive mind-set in order to accomplish goals and rise above adversity.

I realized early on the importance of leadership and the importance of intrinsic motivation as a school safety in elementary school, especially in fourth and fifth grade. I found it rewarding to arrive at school before all other students and help pedestrians and students alike cross busy intersections that connected the school to the community. I was making the school and the world around me a better place.

My family moved a number of times to different sections in Philadelphia. It never interrupted my schooling; I maintained good grades and understood the importance of self-discipline.

During my preadolescent years and beyond in the city of Philadelphia, I observed negative and dysfunctional lifestyles in some neighbors, friends, and family members, but I decided to pursue and emulate the positive role models within and outside my family. I especially was shaped by the behaviors of other positive male influences, such as the neighborhood police officer or the owner of the corner store who worked diligently seven days a week.

I kept an open mind to unfamiliar people and places; I wanted no barriers or limitations to my thinking. Reading about current events allowed me to gain greater exposure to larger issues and forces impacting my life, which accelerated my own social, academic, and emotional growth. Rich debates and conversations with family members and my mother's narratives about her life reinforced values in me that were instilled in her by her grandparents. These too were critical to my personal and educational development.

I understood the importance of seeing beyond my surroundings. Such vision is the connection or energy that feeds planning and preparation. For example, I had to see beyond the efficiency that we lived in for a number of years. I knew our financial status was temporary. Through adversity and perseverance, I was acquiring the tools to be successful: faith, discipline, hard work, positivity, vision, and an open and uncompromising mind-set. I would not allow my mind to think anything was impossible. Clear vision and dedication to excellence enabled me to move forward, succeed, and be the very best that I could be by always giving 100 percent. Most important, I was a role model to my younger sister. I realized at a young age that my mother needed help, especially with regard to my younger sister. Without thinking, I stepped up to the responsibility of making sure that my sister was taken care of when my mother was at work. That meant ensuring that she got home from school safely and completed her homework in a timely fashion, and preparing dinner before my mother arrived home.

Although my family encountered economic hardships, happiness was always plentiful. When living from paycheck to paycheck, one finds joy and importance in seemingly miniscule things. We overcame financial adversity by having a strong faith, trust, love, and reliance on family. Hard times will pull a family apart or bring the members closer together. We all have a choice when it comes to adversity. Our lack of finances never caused our dreams to dry up. We continued to stay positive and work hard every day.

Accessible transportation, movement, and exposure to different areas of the city enabled me to grow and expand my vision. As an older student, I continued my strive to overcome adversity through the power of a positive attitude. I found outlets like joining the band in middle school, where I played the French horn. In high school I gained exposure to many neighborhoods in Philadelphia by playing on the tennis team.

CHALLENGES IN HIGHER EDUCATION

Working my way through college shaped who I am today. I worked at the GAP, at Burger King (only for two weeks), and for William Penn Charter Day Camp in Philadelphia the summer after I completed my freshman year of college. In addition, I spent time mentoring students as a part-time counselor. Collectively, these experiences demonstrated my high level of internal motivation and ability to see beyond immediate limitations. Furthermore, as I reflect on this part of my life, I see that I am the sum of all my experiences and that each situation is temporary. The same is true for you. Life continues to change, so continue to grow and strive for excellence in everything that you do. No job or situation defines who you are as a person on the inside.

I am always asking the question, how did I get here? What did it take to get where I am? This is an interesting question, given that I have not come close to reaching the top professionally and personally. I believe we never truly arrive, but are always being shaped spiritually, personally, and professionally.

I graduated from La Salle University with a bachelor of arts in Political Science. I also graduated from Temple University with a master of arts in Urban Studies and a doctorate in Educational administration. I even spent one year working on a master's in public administration from the University of Delaware, which I did not finish. Academically, I have been fortunate to accomplish a great deal. My overall goal has always been to change the world for the better. As an undergraduate and graduate student, I realized the importance of fostering change in those who came after me. I wanted students to be self-reflective in their pursuit of knowledge, so I worked my way through school by counseling, mentoring, and teaching students. More than anything, I wanted them to ask questions that challenged the status quo or clarified "gray areas" and especially work to recognize and rectify injustices of any kind.

The empowerment of people has always been near and dear to me, and it prompted me to become a trained family mediator after I finished my bachelor's degree. I believed that if families talked and reflected on areas of contention and disagreement, they could develop effective strategies for solving problems. Truancy, curfew, and parent-child respect issues, if left unchecked, could manifest into larger issues, but if caught at the beginning stages could be prevented from escalating to the court system. My training in family mediation and in landlord-tenant disputes allowed me to see that in everything there is a solution, but give-and-take is required.

Earning a doctorate in Educational administration required stamina, determination, and perseverance. When you are working toward a degree, no one cares until you finish. It has been my experience that close is never good enough in our society. Family members and friends often are unable to imagine the laborious process of completing a doctorate. It is not just about taking classes, taking tests, conducting research, and writing a dissertation. I had to learn to navigate the politics and confront academic and financial adversity on my journey to be an expert in this area of study. Few doctoral candidates finish and earn a degree. During this academic pursuit, faculty members on a committee make judgment calls, assess your academic fortitude, and decide whether you are bestowed a degree. Also, one must be open to new ideas and paradigms and have short-term and long-term vision. The completion process required me to master ideas, emotions, attitude, and a work ethic.

My entire life embodies the spirit of MOVEME and represents a tangible example of what you can accomplish with motivation, openness, vision, exposure, mastery, and engagement. Movement of any kind cannot take place without your initiation. We all have limitations, but thinking, dreaming, and envisioning are not among them. We must allow ourselves the opportunity to see beyond what is in front of us and believe that goals and aspirations are worth reaching for in the short- and long-term.

Introduction

The MOVEME Process

We develop ideas that help people to think, reflect, and change.

What do the movie *Groundhog Day* and Nike's motto, "Just Do It," have to do with one another? For starters, there are ideas that tend to stick with you, and then there are those that you wish you could forget. Bill Murray's *Groundhog Day* is symbolic of people's inability to realize that they need to change. In the movie, Bill Murray plays a weatherman who continues to relive the same day over and over again. I pose the question to you: Are you doing the same thing every day but expecting different outcomes or results? How do you break this cycle in your thinking and behavior? If you take the time to reflect on yourself, family, and friends, then you might see that you are stuck or unable to do what is necessary to change your mind-set.

Your mind-set is how you perceive and think about the world and yourself. It can separate greatness from mediocrity, genius from paranoia.

I was in the mall one beautiful day in June and stumbled into a sporting goods and athletic apparel store. I really wasn't looking for anything in particular. I approached an aisle of shirts and saw one with the Nike logo and the words "Just Do It." As I held the shirt closer, I reflected on why people are unable to take those words and apply them to their lives. What does it mean when a person says, "Just do it"? In other words, the person is saying no obstacle will stand in the way of me achieving my goal. This mind-set resonates in sports because individuals and teams are committed to doing everything they can in order to win.

Outside of sports, it is a little harder for individuals to create the urgency and consistency in effort to follow these three words. Moreover, people get side-tracked and become unwilling, unprepared, or unmotivated. They may say they have the mind-set, but they lack the follow-through. In sports, we do not have tolerance for people who lack the skills to compete; we call those who fall into this category losers. However, I believe everyone can be a winner at life if they have the right mind-set and the follow-through. Therefore, I pose the question again: what do *Groundhog Day* and Nike's motto have to do with one another? One speaks to doing things that reinforce the status quo, and the other speaks to change and accomplishing one's goals, no matter how big or small. One tries to change the outcome and the other *replays* it over and over again.

REFLECTION AS A MEANS TO PERSONAL SUCCESS

According to Warren Bennis, "Reflecting on experience is a means of having a Socratic dialogue with yourself, asking the right questions at the right time, in order to discover the truth of yourself and your life. What happened? Why did it happen? What did it mean to me?"[3] Furthermore, "Reflection is a major way in which leaders learn from the past."[4]

---

3   Warren Bennis, *On Becoming a Leader* (New York: Basic Books, 2009), pp. 56–57.
4   Ibid., p. 10.

Regardless of your spiritual or religious beliefs, you cannot deny the fact that your choices determine where you end up in life. Are you intentional in your thinking about life, family, friends, and personal and professional relationships? Can you change things by just reflecting on how to approach a problem rather than accepting the outcome as a foregone conclusion? Can you be better, wiser, or smarter by just realizing a few things in life?

Often we focus only on what we deem are the big decisions and fail to master the art of making well-thought-out small ones. These small choices provide leverage for the big decisions. The small choices are like first downs in football; they move a team closer to the end zone. Some of us, however, score only three points instead of seven. Even more unfortunate is that some of us never score or end up turning the ball over because we are unable or not disciplined enough to put together a drive.

The essence of MOVEME is understanding how to critically make decisions to motivate yourself. More specifically, it provides you with a process that challenges you to engage in self-discovery and reflection in order to transform and reevaluate your thinking so that you see the need and choose to lead when dealing with adverse, potentially life-altering situations.

Once you dedicate yourself to the principles of MOVEME, you should begin to gain a deeper understanding and acquire the thinking skills that promote success in everyday life. What does success look like? The demonstration of personal leadership, the development of tangible solutions, and the ability to foster collaboration and teamwork are examples of success. At the end of the MOVEME process, you will produce written reflections and work samples that shape your job and personal performance.

REFLECTION AS A MEANS TO BETTER LEADERSHIP

Warren Bennis said, "The study of leadership isn't nearly as exact as, say, the study of chemistry. For one thing, the social world isn't nearly as orderly as the physical world, nor is it as susceptible to rules."[5] Leadership is abstract in that when you are dealing with people, you can never be exactly sure as to how they will perceive, think, or behave through a particular situation or event. Therefore, you must be clear in your thinking and confident and true in your convictions. As a leader, you cannot control people's actions like you control the setting in experimental scientific design research (i.e., laboratories). Therefore, people can choose to follow you or not based on very unscientific things.

We see the world, organizations, people, and the mind from the inside out, where thoughts are the driving force from within a person. We cannot see progress unless people are willing to change and confront the things that motivate them personally, intellectually, and professionally. The success and failure of an organization, for instance, is determined by how individuals process the world around them and reflect on the choices and decisions they make, and whether they take leadership over their actions.

President Barack Obama

The historic election of President Barack Obama has highlighted the importance of hope and personal leadership. What we know about the man we have elected to be the first African-American president of the United States is indicative of the kind of reflection, determination, and perseverance we must all bring into our own lives. The following passage in his book *The Audacity of Hope* is indicative of the reflection and determination of President Obama's life:

> It wasn't just the struggles of these men and women that had moved me. Rather, it was their determination, their self-reliance, a relentless optimism in the face of hardship. It brought to

---

5   Ibid., p. xxix.

mind a phrase that my pastor, Rev. Jeremiah A. Wright Jr., had once used in a sermon.[6]

The audacity of hope. That was the best of the American spirit, I thought—having the audacity to believe despite all the evidence to the contrary that we could restore a sense of community to a nation torn by conflict; the gall to believe that despite personal setbacks, the loss of a job or an illness in family or a childhood mired in poverty, we had some control—and therefore responsibility—over our own fate.[7]

I will say this only once: none of us will ever be perfect human beings, but we do have power to make decisions over our lives. The decisions that we make daily help to define our leadership and ultimately give shape to our lives. It is true that our family background, environment, educational status, and value system play a critical part in who we are, but I argue that the decisions and choices we make have an even greater role over how lives turn out. More important, everyone must acknowledge and accept that they have leadership over the decisions they make in the short- and long-term. This has nothing to do with being perfect, but it does impact people positively or negatively as they attempt to make sense of their lives. If we take the time and think even a little about the choices we make, we might end up living happier and healthier lives and even becoming president of the United States one day!

---

6 Barack Obama, *The Audacity of Hope* (New York: Crown Publishers, 2006), p. 356.
7 Ibid.

ECONOMIC INSTABILITY

The instability in the United States and global economies has given MOVEME even more credibility and applicability. No longer can you overcome personal and professional challenges with just financial resources. Since people have lost some or all of their incomes, savings, and retirement, they have had to find other ways to motivate themselves to overcome obstacles. How do you work all your life and do everything right and still find yourself laid off from your job? Many people are realizing that bad things, like losing your job and home, can happen to them even when they have done everything humanly possible to prevent these things from happening.

How do you protect yourself in an unstable economic environment? You need an internal motivational compass that ensures your mind-set stays intact even if the world around you does not. The saying "you must think outside the box" is a survival mind-set that many people find themselves adopting given the scope and impact of the economic downturn. Unfortunately, I know several people who have lost their jobs as a result of layoffs and reduction-in-force measures by state and local governments. After the initial shock of losing employment, many have started to see the need for something deeper and more meaningful to hold onto such as the principles of MOVEME as they try to regroup and reclaim their lives.

EVERYDAY LEADERS IN ACTION

My mother moved my sister and me from North Philadelphia to South Philadelphia during the middle of my third-grade year to improve our living situation and life chances. We moved in with my great-aunt Beulah, who loved life and enjoyed every moment. On my first day at my new school I thought that I knew my way home. We visited the school a day prior to my starting, so I thought I would be fine getting to and from school. Unfortunately, I was half right and made it to school with no problem, but I did not make it home as easily. I left Childs Elementary School like every other student, but I went in the wrong direction. Anyone who has visited South Philadelphia knows that the streets and blocks look very similar and the landmarks are the corner stores, which are on every other block.

I thought every street was my new address, but two hours later I realized this was not the case. I walked into corner store after corner store only to find that each was not the correct landmark. Eventually someone in the store asked me if I was lost and I said yes! The Italian man who worked in the store seemed to show genuine concern for my well-being. He asked me twice what my address was, and I said, "1118 Tasker Street."

South Philadelphia was residentially segregated in the 1970's, with Italian-Americans living on the east side of Broad Street and African-American livings on the west side. Guess which side of Broad Street I found myself on? The Italian man checked the address and stated in the most polite manner that I could not live at 1118 Tasker Street because no blacks lived on that street, much less in the neighborhood. What he did after that was a blur, but the essence of everyday leadership.

The gentleman called Childs Elementary, explained the situation to the administrators, and found out my correct address. It was not 1118 Tasker Street but 1811 Tasker Street. Switching the house number was just a small mistake on my part, really! The gentleman took me home in his car to my new address. Aunt Beulah thanked him, and I thanked him for everything that he had done. I wish I knew this gentleman's name so I could have thanked him later on in life. He demonstrated the kind of everyday leadership that I wish all people would demonstrate. He did not get an award or written up in a newspaper. He didn't play basketball, was not a politician, and was not famous. When you think of all the bad things that could have happened to me, that man's actions illustrate the level of courage and leadership we must take the time to demonstrate when the opportunity presents itself. This is just one example of many throughout my life where people demonstrated everyday leadership.

MOVEME is shaped by how people develop and implement strategies for taking leadership over the decisions they make in their lives. There are no easy answers, and our thinking may have to undergo a transformation in order to be where we aspire to be in life. How fast we get there will be determined by how we address and confront our internal self and our willingness to reexamine our mind-set and actions.

Ultimately, MOVEME is not about the end result or finished product, but about the planning and processes that lead to the finished product. Therefore, you never fully arrive at your destination; you always keep doing things that encourage you to ask yourself, "What will MOVEME?"

CHAPTER 1

GETTING STARTED ON SELF-REFLECTION

Do not go where the path may lead:
Go instead where there is no path
And leave a trail.
—Ralph Waldo Emerson

If you do not spend time devoted to thinking about the choices and decisions you make, you are preventing personal, professional, and spiritual growth. Many people accept life at face value and believe or behave as if their thoughts do not contribute to their reality. It is easier for them to blame others for their reality.

This chapter examines the power of knowing as we journey down the path of life. We are all traveling in many directions as we attempt to find happiness, success, and personal and professional fulfillment. What is the best course of action? How do we get there? Can we follow someone else's blueprint for our own lives? Do we have the courage to find and develop our own pathway?

These are just some of the questions that we must address if we are to have the kind of life that we need or desire.

It is easy to be a follower and to want to know what is around the corner—always. We are unable to predict the future, of course, but we must stay the course. There is no common or universal blueprint for our lives. It is our own responsibility to navigate life's ups and downs. The quote by Ralph Waldo Emerson above illustrates both the uncertainty and opportunity that we are presented with when we make decisions. In making our own decisions, we chart a course that prepares us for the future. These decisions may mean deviating from what family and friends think is the "right" path for our lives.

ASSESS YOUR STATE OF MIND

Who determines the right path for you?

_____

_____

_____

_____

_____

_____

Are you afraid to create your own path? Why?

_____

_____

_____

_____

_____

_____

How many pathways have you created?

_____

_____

_____

_____

_____

_____

Have you experienced U-turns or obstacles? Explain.

_____

_____

_____

_____

_____

_____

Have you run out gas? Why?

_____

_____

_____

_____

_____

_____

Have you been disillusioned by the consequences of your decisions? How so?

_____

_____

_____

_____

_____

_____

These questions allow you to reflect on and analyze your actions and decisions. How often do you think about your choices? Sometimes it seems like the only ones reflecting on life, relationship, politics, and learning are late-night and popular comedians like David Letterman, Jay Leno, and Chris Rock. Unfortunately, we are not trying to create our own pathways to success, but we want everything figured out for us at the outset. Life would be simpler if our futures were predetermined from the outset. We would like to believe that our "cheese" will never be moved, as author Dr. Spencer Johnson, in the transformative and awe-inspiring book *Who Moved My Cheese?*, elaborates on how human beings negotiate, avoid, confront, and overcome their fear of change from a personal and professional standpoint.

The game of checkers and chess is based on critical-thinking skills. The game of checkers is based on being quick, forward-thinking, and developing strategies to outmaneuver your opponent in order to win a match. Comparatively speaking, the game of chess requires another level of intense analytical and strategic thinking and rewards players for being methodical and developing strategies to anticipate your opponents' moves well in advance. In retrospect, both board games have one thing in common; you must weigh all possible outcomes before you make a move. Many people move with little or no data, or even outdated data. What is your mental approach to achieving success? This is just one question to pose to yourself.

ASSESS YOUR STATE OF MIND

Another way to analyze your life is viewing it as a race to be run. Are you a sprinter in your thoughts and aspirations, often only considering the immediate or short-term goals you need to achieve, or are you a long-distance runner who sees the big picture and trains for the long haul?

Are you a chess or checkers kind of person? Why do you see yourself as this type of player?

_____

_____

_____

_____

_____

_____

Do you see life more from a sprinter's perspective or from a long-distance runner's? Explain.

_____

_____

_____

_____

_____

What is your level of preparation (physical, mental, intellectual, etc.) to enter the race?

_____

_____

_____

_____

_____

_____

CHAPTER 2

THE BUILDING BLOCKS OF THE
LEADERSHIP PYRAMID

"Our thinking is always under construction."

If we approach our thinking as construction workers approach their work, we would understand that there is always room for growth and learning. Although construction projects have end dates and buildings eventually are finished, our thinking and who we are as individuals will never end if we understand the development of personal growth.

The majority of people are led to believe that once they achieve professional and academic greatness, they have "arrived" at their destination of being all-knowing. However, one can never "arrive," since learning is a continuous process. We need to be at a stage of personal development where we reflect on our thinking and the actions that have come as a result. There are different parts to our thinking that are challenged only through understanding the choices that we make, analyzing our mind-set, using reflection as a tool for self-improvement, and assuming positive leadership over our lives.

THE MOVEME SELF-IMPROVEMENT & LEADERSHIP PYRAMID

The MOVEME Self-Improvement and Leadership Pyramid holds the key to self-improvement. The leadership pyramid provides a visual aid that allows us to see the complex nature of making decisions and how it impacts the choices we make in our daily lives. In developing this pyramid, I realized that we must address all quadrants if we are to be successful in our pursuits.

The reflection triangle teaches us to process whether the decisions we make are actually working. It is difficult to have a healthy and open mind-set if we are not reflecting on our experiences, both good and bad. If we analyze the right bottom quadrant, we see that choices are a direct result of reflection; it impacts choices you make in your everyday life. At the top of the pyramid is leadership, which provides the motivation for the action needed to generate positive change. These quadrants are interrelated. For example, if you are making poor choices, it impacts your mind-set in negative ways. If you continue to make poor choices, you start to question your abilities and self-esteem and eventually undermine your confidence in the decisions you make.

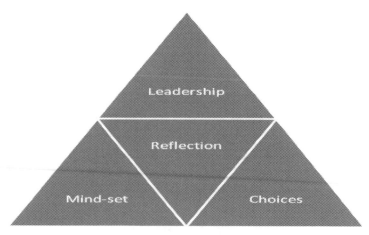

ASSESS YOUR STATE OF MIND

What does this pyramid say to you?

_____

_____

_____

_____

_____

If you were to create your own pyramid using the same triangles—
leadership, reflection, mind-set, and choices—would the triangles
stay the same or would you reposition them?

_____

_____

_____

_____

_____

_____

When was the last time you reflected on the personal choices you
have made?

_____

_____

_____

_____

_____

When was the last time you reflected on the professional choices you have made?

_____

_____

_____

_____

_____

Have you reflected enough to determine if what you did actually materialized?

_____

_____

_____

_____

If you are not making wise choices, then what is your mind-set?

_____

_____

_____

_____

Can you have a healthy mind-set if you are not making good choices? Why or why not?

_____

_____

_____

_____

Are the choices you are making professionally guided by some form of data?

_____

_____

_____

_____

_____

_____

Collectively, list five professional, educational, and personal goals you have for yourself.

_____

_____

_____

_____

_____

What are some of the bridges you must cross in order to accomplish your stated goals? What other factors must you consider?

_____

_____

_____

_____

_____

What are some of the *internal* (mental, thoughts, decisions) challenges you must confront in order to cross over your bridges? What type of thinking and action is required to cross safely?

_____

_____

_____

_____

_____

_____

What are some *external* (external forces) challenges you must confront in order to cross over your bridges? What type of thinking and action is required to cross safely?

_____

_____

_____

_____

_____

_____

Are you intellectually, emotionally, physically, and spiritually equipped enough to cross the bridge?

_____

_____

_____

_____

_____

_____

Can you approach each bridge in the same manner? Why or why not?

_____

_____

_____

_____

_____

_____

Have you been able to help friends or family members cross any educational, professional, or personal bridges?

_____

_____

_____

_____

_____

A GUIDING THOUGHT TO PONDER

By utilizing the MOVEME (Motivation, Openness, Vision, Exposure, Mastery, and Engagement) process of leadership, you will be able to build strategies for overcoming personal limitations, which undermine your ability to help youth, families, and yourself. Only by reflecting on your mind-set can you make adjustments to your attitude and the amount of effort you channel to crossing bridges to reaching your goals.

There is no recipe for being an effective leader, but if you ask yourself constructive, surface-penetrating, and solution-oriented questions, they will lead you in the right direction. In the book, *QBQ! The Question Behind the Question*, John Miller states that we can make better decisions in life by reflecting and posing deeper and richer questions to ourselves. His argument is that we are accountable for our actions and choices, and if we discipline our minds by resisting the temptation to ask negative-outcome questions, we can eventually reap the benefits of a positive mind-set. The following list provides examples of the kinds of questions you should ask yourself.

MOTIVATION

What motivates you?

_____

_____

_____

_____

_____

_____

What feeds your internal motivation?

_____

_____

_____

_____

_____

_____

OPENNESS

Are you honest with yourself about any (judgmental) attitudes and limitations?

_____

_____

_____

_____

_____

_____

Are you open in your thoughts, behaviors, and ideas about people different than you? How do you demonstrate this to others?

_____

_____

_____

_____

_____

VISION

What is your personal/professional short-term and long-term plan for the future?

_____

_____

_____

_____

_____

Are you vision-impaired (lacking a vision)? If so, why do you think that is?

_____

_____

_____

_____

_____

What do you want to be doing professionally in five to ten years?

_____

_____

_____

_____

_____

_____

Are your current job tasks moving you closer to reaching your professional goals?

_____

_____

_____

_____

_____

_____

Is your current job and passion one and the same? If not, what must you do to make that happen?

_____

_____

_____

_____

_____

_____

EXPOSURE

Are you exposed to people who encourage you to reinforce the status quo or challenge it?

_____

_____

_____

_____

_____

_____

Are you making better and more informed decisions about your professional and personal life based on your exposure to diverse ideas?

_____

_____

_____

_____

_____

_____

MASTERY

Have you committed yourself to excellence in your thinking and practice? If so, provide examples.

_____

_____

_____

_____

_____

_____

When was the last time you learned from a negative situation professionally? What did you learn?

_____

_____

_____

_____

_____

ENGAGEMENT

Do you know how to communicate in a manner where you get the results you want?

_____

_____

_____

_____

_____

Are you able to listen to people when you disagree with them? What strategies do you employ to do this effectively?

_____

_____

_____

_____

_____

Do you have the ability to develop a mind-set that helps people overcome personal obstacles?

_____

_____

_____

_____

_____

_____

How do you know that this mind-set is working?

_____

_____

_____

_____

_____

How do you build trusting relationships with people?

_____

_____

_____

_____

_____

A GUIDING THOUGHT TO PONDER

Never be afraid to fail. Those five words should drive your life.

I was watching a segment of *60 Minutes* with Steve Kroft in which he interviewed LeBron James, one the best NBA players ever. It was a very uplifting, empowering, and engaging look into the how the twenty-six-year-old has become a household name. One of the most powerful things he said was that you cannot be afraid to fail at anything. Given what this young African-American male has gone through in his life—when he was growing up, he and his mother had to endure living from place to place because of financial and family instability—his words resonated as if he were a wise old man.

The fact is that many people are afraid of failure and live their lives unable to make choices that will take them to the next level of personal development. They remain in watching rather than doing status, content with being "good enough" and never reaching their true and unique potential. Everything *is* easier said than done, but doing is what separates the men from the boys. Whether you admit it or not, you learn when you make mistakes. The majority of people succumb to their fears of failure and avoidance of mistakes. Yes, there are times when you can learn from others who have made mistakes.

ASSESS YOUR STATE OF MIND

Sometimes you have to fail at something to get to the situation that is best for you. Have there been any situations when you were afraid to fail?

_____
_____
_____
_____
_____
_____

What have you failed at in your life? What did you learn about yourself in your failure?

_____
_____
_____
_____
_____
_____

Chapter 3

Time Spent on Reflection

"You are a reflection of the time you have put into yourself."

The word *reflection* is so overused that people misconstrue its meaning and believe it is something to be avoided. The goal of this chapter is for you to understand the value and complexity of taking time for thinking, observing, and self-analysis. In addition, this chapter also addresses the unspoken but elusive role that time has in our lives. Although most people understand the significance of time, we need to figure out our level of awareness about the role it has in how we see relationships, people, and ourselves.

What does your reflection say about you? Is your reflection true or deceptive?

_____

_____

_____

_____

_____

_____

Through this process of revelation we examine and understand our progression or regression. Some of us are afraid to see that real person in the mirror or hold ourselves under a microscope. But this reflection is necessary because it forces us to take into account how we became the individual we are today.

Do you know how others perceive you? How can you answer this question if you do not take time each day to think about your actions in the short-term and long-term and the impact of them? When people say they do not care what others think of them, are they fooling themselves?

Do you allow the world a window into your true self, or are you a walking smokescreen of deception? Such deception is the result of your inability to reflect on who you are. Honest self-reflection is not always kind. It can hurt your spirit and cause greater internal turmoil initially.

The fact is you are only as good as the time you have put into yourself. Many people neglect themselves and never put the time into reaching their true potential.

It's been said that time is money. We get the sense that time is a valuable commodity and that we should reflect on how important it is to our existence. Dr. Bantikassegn Workalemahu offered another view of time: "Time is life." When I first heard this, I had to stop and really think about what time is and the meaning that I place on it. Utilizing time effectively provides me an opportunity to think through personal and professional decisions. When you define *time* from that context it changes your reality of what you have done with your life. You must reflect on how you have used or misused time. One truth is a constant about time: time is not retrievable once it is lost. In theory we can lose money and regain it through work and labor, education, lottery winnings, inheritance, investments, or other financial undertakings. But time is elusive in many ways because people have not understood the value of it as it relates to their life. Time denotes the fragility of our existence and determines and measures our overall existence on earth. As humans, we bring relevance to time through actions, conditions, mind-sets, and memories. Although time is elusive, it is a way for us to describe days, hours, birth, life, and death.

Many of us have spent precious time on earth by working incessantly rather than focusing on what really matters. We cannot get life back. We must reflect on family and friends and think about how we are spending our precious commodity. We must be intentional about the time we have with one another and take advantage of every moment that we are afforded. Let's not squander it on petty arguments that have little meaning in the grand scheme of life.

ASSESS YOUR STATE OF MIND

How do you define *time*?

_____
_____
_____
_____
_____
_____
_____

Are you unable to manage your time? If so, why do you think that is?

_____

_____

_____

_____

_____

_____

Are you a procrastinator?

_____

_____

_____

_____

_____

_____

What must you do to take control of your time?

_____

_____

_____

_____

_____

_____

CHAPTER 4

MOTIVATION: BE INTENTIONAL

This chapter poses two important questions. What do you do in a deliberate and purposeful manner? What are the thoughts behind your actions? You must always devote time to thinking through your action in order to produce the kind of result you want in life. Some people do not give focused thought (pure energy) and effort to their actions, which is the heart of being intentional. The intent is the heart!

Being intentional can be defined as having mental discipline over our actions and thoughts. What is any more intentional than a handshake? When you initiate the act of giving a handshake, you generate energy to the impending exchange of physical energy. It is meant to communicate a feeling of confidence and communication from human to human. You are deliberate in your action, which is transferred to the next person. Conversely, a weak handshake conveys a lack of energy, thought, and life. In the book *The Hidden Messages in Water,* author Masaru Emoto says there is power in words we speak, whether intentional or not. In his research with ice crystals and water, he concluded that the vibration of good words had a positive impact on ice crystals and the vibration from negative words had a detrimental impact. Emoto asserted that "the entire universe is in a state of vibration, and each thing generates its own frequency, which is unique."[8]

There are times in life when you realize that you are on the right path and that your thinking is pushing you in the right direction. This chapter happens to be one of them. I started writing this chapter on the power of intentionality in March 2009 and found a book on the power of intention four months later. *The Power of Intention* provides legitimacy not only to this chapter but to my thinking. Dr. Wayne Dyer states that intention is much greater than free will or ego, which looks to material rewards and achievements as validation:

> [I]ntention is being presented in this book as an invisible energy field that is inherent in all physical form, intention, then is a part of the inexplicable, nonmaterial world of Spirit. Spirit eludes our attempts to explain and define it because it's a dimension beyond beginnings and ends, beyond boundaries, beyond symbols, and beyond form itself.[9]

What causes a dream to become reality, or more specifically, what moves the abstract to the concrete (philosophy to practice)? Do you learn something by just letting it happen, or does it take actual effort and focused energy and emotions around that particular goal or event for it to take shape? You must possess and practice intentionality in order to rise.

I propose that there is a point where thinking and action meet and together produce desired impact. The key is the type of effort exerted to complete that particular task. Nothing happens by chance, so we must be cognizant of the energy we manifest through thinking; this determines our approach to life, relationships, and

8   Masaru Emoto, *The Hidden Messages in Water* (New York: Atria Books, 2001), p. 39.
9   Wayne Dyer, *The Power of Intention* (New York: Hay House, 2004), p. 22.

personal growth. The next step is to channel that mental energy into something concrete. According to Leo Weidner, in the book *The Slight Edge*, "the thoughts you allow on the stage of your mind create energy and messages that are transferred to people around you."[10] It is a mental challenge for a person to take something as abstract as a dream and make it real. How many things have you taken out of the dream realm and made real?

I think people make a choice to be unintentional but hope for intentional results. Very rarely do people get what they want when they do not give the full effort consistently to achieve a particular goal. It is difficult to determine through a scale if a person is highly motivated. Motivation is determined by action and thought. We see examples of this in the world of sports, where athletes dedicate their mind and body to accomplish one specific goal. Much like capturing your thoughts in a diary, the intentionality chart provides an opportunity to document whether you are moving in the direction of or away from achieving your personal and professional goals.

INTENTIONALITY CHART

The chart provides an opportunity to document the choices you make throughout the week and what happens as a result. It is also meant to encourage you to keep a working diary of your thinking because if it is not tracked, it can lead to unforeseen consequences in your life. The chart demonstrates where you were proactive and the decisions and choices you prioritized during the course of the week. In order to transform your reality, you must document examples of when you have fulfilled the seven intentionality points through his daily practice. So a person may ask himself, "How was I proactive today?" "Where is the evidence that I made something a priority?" "How was I productive?" "What did I practice on that made me a better person?" "How did I demonstrate persistence?" "How were my thoughts positive in nature?"

---

10 Leo Weidner, *The Slight Edge* (Springville, Utah: Cedar Fort Inc., 2008), p. 20.

- Mediocrity + My Dreams = False Sense of Reality

- Positive Thoughts + Positive Actions + My Dreams = The Reality That I Want

Abstract to Concrete: 7 Points Must Be Followed Daily (Intentionality Chart)

	SUN-DAY	MON-DAY	TUES-DAY-	WED-NESDAY	THURS-DAY	FRI-DAY	SATUR-DAY
PROACTIVE							
PRIORITY							
PREPARE							
PRODUCTIVE							
PRACTICE							
PERSISTENCE							
POSITIVE							

ASSESS YOUR STATE OF MIND

How did you demonstrate intentionality this week?

_____

_____

_____

_____

_____

_____

If your motivation is driven by your heart and energy, how much are you providing to achieving your goals?

_____

_____

_____

_____

_____

_____

What are you doing to change your level of intentionality? If nothing, why?

_____

_____

_____

_____

_____

Did something change in your daily practice as a result of charting your events?

_____

_____

_____

_____

_____

A GUIDING THOUGHT TO PONDER

Michael Jordan was always intentional when he was on the basketball court. We saw his passion, attitude, work ethic, swagger, attention to excellence, and effort all working collectively to help him win six NBA championships. One could almost feel his will to win a basketball game even before he stepped on the court.

In football, Tom Brady, quarterback of the New England Patriots, also exuded intentionality in his demeanor while leading his team to three Super Bowl victories. He has confidence, attitude, and an assassin-like accuracy that makes fans take note and say, "This guy believes that he can beat you even before you play him."

CHAPTER 5

THE POWER OF MUSIC, VISUAL ARTS & PICTURES: I AM WHAT I HEAR AND SEE

A young lady once told me that ancient Chinese civilizations believed that music was medicine for the soul. —Anonymous

In this chapter we examine the connection between the types of music people are exposed to and the decisions they make in their everyday life, if such a connection exists. Does music help you grow and view the world differently than a person who listens to another type of music? What music drives you? Are you smooth jazz, reggae, Latin, or hip-hop?

Diversity of music equals the level of diversity in people, in my estimation. Have you ever met people who listen to only one type of music? They seem so one-dimensional in their outlook and approach to life. However, if you have an ear for all types of music, you probably find it easy to interact with people of other ethnic and racial groups and different generations.

I grew up in the 1980s with many musical influences, including hip-hop, smooth jazz, reggae, rhythm and blues, gospel, pop, Latin salsa, hard rock, and classical. The untimely death of Michael Jackson, "the King of Pop," reminded me of the power that music has to move people to do wonderful and beautiful acts for mankind. Through many of his lyrics people were exposed to the value of diversity and helping people who are less fortunate than they are.

Everyone needs to find out what is at the core of who they are, and a good starting place is understanding the type of music that fuels their mind and heart. I consider myself a smooth jazz type on the outside and a hip-hop and rhythm and blues guy in my soul. We fail to see that the music we listen to speaks to various parts of our inner self. When I analyze myself, I see that on the exterior I am laid back and mellow in my approach to dealing with people, but I am a perfectionist when it comes to accomplishing my goals, which I attribute to the hip-hop music that I grew up listening to that inspired me to be the best. My rhythm and blues side is the wisdom and knowledge I gain from respecting people and life.

Why is music relevant to life? Think about a great song and how it makes you feel at any given moment. It can set the tone for the entire day and make you feel invincible. In many ways it is therapeutic to the mind and helps you get in touch with your feelings.

Music helps drive your emotions. Sometimes I need something positive and uplifting; other times I need something a little street and edgy. Currently, I am listening to some smooth jazz by Boney James and some '80s rap from Whodini. They offer me a positive alternative to my reality. I am remembering a happy time when I was a teenager and trying to stay mellow.

ASSESS YOUR STATE OF MIND

What kind of music makes you who you are?

_____

_____

_____

_____

_____

_____

Is music therapeutic for you?

_____

_____

_____

_____

_____

Does it provide an escape from reality?

_____

_____

_____

_____

_____

Can you use music to drive you in your everyday life?

_____

_____

_____

_____

_____

The Power of Pictures

Some people are more visual than others and can identify more quickly with pictures and diagrams than with written words. In addition, people can be motivated through pictures and graphic representations. A picture captures a moment in time and can elicit emotions and help you transcend where you are if you allow your mind to take you there, much like a particular song. In *The Power of Intention*, Dr. Wayne Dyer describes the power of photographs:

> You may find it difficult to believe that photography is a form of energy reproduction and that every photograph contains energy. See for yourself by strategically placing photographs taken in moments of happiness, love, and receptivity to spiritual help around your living quarters, in your workplace, in your automobile, and even on your clothing or in your pocket or wallet.[11]

Clip art bridges the abstract and makes it concrete to the reader. Using clip art is like being an artist and having a canvas; you are free to create and interpret it directly from your mind and soul.

---

11 Wayne Dyer, *The Power of Intention* (New York: Hay House, Inc., 2004), p. 76.

CHAPTER 6

OPENNESS: ARE YOU A PRISONER?

Many things affect our freedom as thinkers. We are imprisoned by others who keep our minds from growing immeasurably and unchallenged. We are unchallenged when we do not question the implications and impact—negative or positive—of our decisions. As a result, many people are confined by their perceptions, attitudes, and internal mental maps of the world around them.

This is an intriguing question to pose to yourself or a friend. Are you a prisoner of your own thinking? If so, how did this happen? Why did this happen? I assert that being a prisoner of your own thinking means being safe in the decisions that you make. More specifically, it means not taking any calculated risks or gambles in the professional choices you make. You pick the known over the unknown, which may have come as a result of your experiences and upbringing. This prevents you from becoming the best you can be or believing that your passions can be a reality. This has implications for your happiness in the short-term and long-term.

In addition, your level of happiness is directly influenced by whether you are imprisoned by your thinking. Our parents

35

had their own ideas, survival tendencies, and approaches, which may still serve us well today. Life lessons are passed down from generation to generation. However, some of us never break out of the shackles of the habits, perceptions, attitudes, or mindset that trap us in mediocrity and paralysis. Are the negative behaviors and toxic thinking that hamper our growth personally and professionally passed down to us also? Many of us have gained exposure to different thinking by way of technology, friends, education, and our own personal growth, and as a result we question how things were done by previous generations and reject the toxic thinking that has been handed down to us.

It was thought at one point that the best course in life was to go to school, get a job, remain at that job for thirty years or so, and then retire. That was the mind-set of a previous generation because that was appropriate at that time given the economic, political, and social conditions. However, applying 1960's thinking and approaches to many of the economic and social problems in 2010 may not necessarily work.

According to Dr. Wayne Dyer, "you'll find your passion in what inspires you the most."[12] Too many people sacrifice their God-given talents and passions in life. They have sold out on themselves and resigned themselves to a life of what could've, what should've, and what would've been if only they had not gotten sidetracked, or had a family, or met this person, or lost that job. We use laundry lists of excuses to cover up the fact that we have allowed situations in life to dictate where we are today rather than readjusting our thinking and trying again so we can truly live out our passions.

---

12   Wayne Dyer, 10 Secrets for Success and Inner Peace (New York: Hay House, 2002), p.8

ASSESS YOUR STATE OF MIND

Are you able to change with the times and adjust your thinking, or are you trapped in your thinking for what worked years ago?

_____

_____

_____

_____

_____

What do you do when your elders are able to provide you with only past experiences and not current factual information? How do you handle this disconnect?

_____

_____

_____

_____

_____

Do you listen to, reflect, and challenge what your elders tell you, or do you blindly accept perceptions that are passed down from one generation to the next?

_____

_____

_____

_____

_____

Are you a prisoner of past failures and personal defeats ?

_____

_____

_____

_____

_____

If you answered yes to the previous question, how did you handle it?

_____

_____

_____

_____

_____

A GUIDING THOUGHT TO PONDER

At some point we become a prisoner of our parents' thinking if we do not spend time reflecting on whether their thinking and behavior is still relevant. We must always love and show our parents and grandparents respect and honor, but we must still question their worldview so that we do not become imprisoned by their unfulfilled dreams and aspirations. Some us are prisoners and do not even know that we are. We continue to react and behave in the same manner.

Chapter 7

Vision: Are You Able to See Around Adversity & Obstacles?

This chapter provides the foundation for understanding how important vision is to us in accomplishing our stated goals or purpose in life. Without an adequate map for our professional or personal lives, we are destined to go in the wrong direction or never reach our destination.

Millions of people spend their days and lives without a vision. Where does vision come from, and what drives it? How do we know when to change directions if one direction is taking us off the appropriate course?

In order to have crystal clear vision, we must take the time to determine what our goals are in the short-term and long-term. These can be professional, personal, academic, or just daily goals. In developing goals, we must do some homework and figure out what is needed to accomplish those goals. Unfortunately, many people believe that some goals are unattainable and therefore they convince themselves not to try. Some goals are meant for you and some are not. The only way to find out which ones are for you is to engage in proper personal and professional planning and give all your positive energy and attitude toward this undertaking. Not too many people give their best effort and dedicate themselves enough to completing their goals. Once you have determined what your goals are, then your vision starts to become clearer:

Diligence + Planning + Goals = Vision

When I am expected to go to an unfamiliar destination, whether to see friends or family or for a job interview, I often get lost or turned around. I think it is my nature to get lost even when I have MapQuest directions! Eventually, I get to my destination. To compensate for my propensity to get lost, I either visit where I am going the day before or leave for my destination early enough so that I account for getting lost. In life we can get on the wrong track and still recover. Many times it is meant for us to take the scenic route to our destination rather than the straight and narrow. We end up learning something about ourselves in the process through whatever ordeals and tribulations we must endure while going in that direction. Even when we are traveling east when we should be going west, we should still reflect on our experiences, ask questions, and think through conflict, weighing the consequences of our actions, and then assess and reassess our short-term and long-term goals. We are concerned more with the intentional process rather than the end result. Only two types of people fail at this activity: those who do not try and those who do not reflect. Many people stand on the sidelines and tell people which direction they should proceed without knowing where they are going. It's hard to follow what they are saying because they don't take their own advice on how to live life. So when they say go north, on what are they basing their data?

ASSESS YOUR STATE OF MIND

Who or what is directing your life?

_____

_____

_____

_____

_____

What hard choices have you had to make personally or professionally?

_____

_____

_____

_____

_____

What are some of the outcomes of those choices? Have they moved you closer to or pushed you away from your goals?

_____

_____

_____

_____

_____

A GUIDING THOUGHT TO PONDER

"The only way for students to overcome the shortcomings of their parents is for them to take the lead in their own future."

Who determines your future when you are a child? Our parents have a large say in where we end up as adults. I was raised to believe that our parents know best and have the requisite child-rearing skills to help us to become the best we can be. Most parents do the best they can do, but sometimes we take on some of the same negative patterns, attitudes, and mind-sets that have imprisoned their lives. At some point we must challenge ourselves and take leadership over our own choices even if it brings growing pains. There comes a point—and it's different for each person—when you can no longer blame your parents for the mistakes you make in life.

CHAPTER 8

EXPOSURE: WHAT IS SHAPING YOUR WORLDVIEW?

"How one views the world is everything, but we must be willing to open our minds first."

Avoid limited exposure. You cannot allow yourself to think only inside the box and see the world through just one lens. The desire to see beyond your family, community, city, state, and country gives you the ability to be a deeper thinker and more informed individual.

Diversity in exposure leads to diversity of thought, which are key ingredients to our growth personally and professionally. We must always be aware of economic, political, and social forces shaping our thinking. We must become good listeners who synthesize information and challenge it when statements cannot be supported or substantiated.

In *The Secret*, Rhonda Byrne described how what we are exposed to affects our thinking: "Everything that's coming into your life you are attracting into your life. And it's attracted to you by virtue of the images you're holding in your mind. It's what you're thinking. Whatever is going on in your mind you are attracting to you."[13] We are the sum of our thoughts, and we are attracting things and people to us without our knowledge. Therefore, if you think positive thoughts, you are more inclined to bring people and situations into your world that have positive outcomes. Conversely, if you are negative, you are more likely to (unknowingly) attract people who feel the same way you do. Your thoughts are like mini energy bursts you put into the universe.

ASSESS YOUR STATE OF MIND

Do you consider yourself a positive or negative thinker?

_____

_____

_____

_____

_____

_____

Are you more inclined to be a positive thinker? Why?

_____

_____

_____

_____

_____

_____

---

13   Rhonda Byrne, *The Secret* (New York: Atria Books, 2006), p. 4.

Are you inclined to be a negative thinker? Why?

_____

_____

_____

_____

_____

ARE YOU AN ISLAND OR A BRIDGE?

Often we give the appearance of being connected to people's feelings, perceptions, and attitudes, but in reality we are an island surrounded by water. We need to look inside to see if we are building positive relationships. Instead of an island, we can be a bridge that connects with others about our common external and internal needs.

Organizationally and professionally, you can never be an island. When we think of an island, we imagine beautiful palm trees and tropical breezes and gorgeous blue water as far as the eye can see. We do not see the stranded person who is waving the white flag, hoping to be rescued. Being an island means that you are not open to the world around you. You lack exposure to ideas and processes that may challenge your worldview.

To be an island is to think inwardly and to perceive the world from just one lens rather than from a kaleidoscope. To be an island is to lack exposure and view competition rather than collaboration as an approach to group processes. Islands are nice places to visit, but they are temporary places of comfort and foster isolation in one's thinking.

A bridge conjures up a perception of people crossing from one place to another. It provides a sense of safety and accomplishment, which leads to an even greater self-awareness. Bridges can be stable and strong or weak and long, so we must make sure that if we are a bridge for someone we are strong and resistant to any shock (loss of income, loss of a home, sickness) to our foundation.

ASSESS YOUR STATE OF MIND

Do you consider yourself an island or bridge?

_____

_____

_____

_____

_____

What does it mean to be on an island?

_____

_____

_____

_____

_____

If you are a bridge, where are the pressure points (obstacles) in your thinking?

_____

_____

_____

_____

_____

If you are an island, does your thinking need to be rescued?

_____

_____

_____

_____

_____

A bridge allows people or vehicles to cross an obstacle. Families and close friends have to cross bridges every day. Their obstacles could be personal, environmental, school-based, or simply the result of poor life choices.

Sometimes people become islands when they are rebuked by others. It's easy to become isolated and detached from others mentally, physically, and emotionally for various reasons. In many ways, the bridge provides connectivity of the mind and body and allows a person to reach out to other individuals in the same manner. Bridges can take all shapes and sizes to an individual. The barriers that prevent you from reaching a person might be physical or mental, but either way they must be crossed successfully.

A Guiding Thought to Ponder

"If you think you can cross the bridge, you will cross it."

Before making choices, we must ask and answer pertinent questions. Being reflective forces us to overcome obstacles, which may require us to cross steep, narrow, long, and weak bridges. Another fact is that we must cross bridges in our thinking in order to accomplish our goals.

A bridge could represent a troubled home life or a troubled state of mind. Start by identifying what type of bridge it is. Is it a long, short, stable, or well-lit bridge? Is it a bridge filled with cracks over treacherous water leading to nowhere? Once you identify what kind of bridge you are, then you can start to develop strategies for strengthening your foundation. This may mean reaching out to others for help or reflecting on areas of weakness in order to change your mind-set.

Chapter 9

Mastery: Growth and Evaluation

"Excellence is the byproduct of a good attitude and work habits, which work hand in hand. Indifference to preparation and shortcutting the mechanics of excellence are signs of mediocrity."

We see this truth played out in sports all the time: when a good attitude and good habits unite, the result is usually excellence. It's easy to witness this when watching a football or basketball game. In everyday life, however, this union is not always so evident. If you look for it, you can find it. I see examples of this when a mechanic works on my car, when a plumber fixes a broken pipe in my house, or when a doctor prescribes medicine for me.

As humans, we are always in a hurry to do something. The need to accomplish goals forces us to bypass the long and straight or sometimes winding road. We live in a society that is time- and deadline-driven. Against this reality we attempt to fast-forward learning and, as a result, excellence. Excellence is being the best at what you try to accomplish in life.

But what happens when you shortcut a particular process? How can you be the best if you are not mechanically sound in your approach? You miss the little things that promote and strengthen success. I am reminded of the martial arts movies I grew up watching and the level of dedication that was required by the student in order to reach the next level of mastery. In one scene, the student had to hold an egg in his outstretched hand for hours without breaking it. On the surface, it seemed like a waste of time and had no relevance to the task at hand. However, the goal was to become excellent at a particular martial arts technique. Little did the student know that he was building mental and physical strength, and discipline at the same time.

ASSESS YOUR STATE OF MIND

Are you good at making people around you better? If so, how?

_____

_____

_____

_____

_____

Have you ever been part of a team? Did you make it better? How?

_____

_____

_____

_____

_____

What intangibles did you bring to the team?

_____

_____

_____

_____

_____

_____

Do you rely on quantifiable measures to determine if you are making a difference within an organization?

_____

_____

_____

_____

_____

_____

Name a time when you took a shortcut to success. Did it pay off or backfire?

_____

_____

_____

_____

_____

_____

GUIDING THOUGHT TO PONDER

There are human qualities we cannot measure with a scale, computer, or ruler, but they are just as important to the success and failure of a person as those things that we can touch and measure, such as a car, a salary, or one's height. We are attempting to understand the value these unquantifiable characteristics add to our lives. We know that they are important, but we fail to assign them the importance that more tangible things in life warrant.

Attitude, leadership, integrity, character, and trust are critical elements to the success of any organization. Yes, a person can be good at his or her job and still be without these personal and professional qualities. In *My Dream Map*, John Maxwell states that "character flaws can prevent you from achieving success."[14] The 2008 housing collapse in the United States and the financial collapse here and globally showed that many people conducted business without demonstrating many of these qualities. We see people who are good at what they do but who act as if integrity, trust, and positive leadership do not matter. Our society has become more concerned with the metrics of success than the intangible, immeasurable qualities that contribute to the success or failure of an organization.

We must hold individuals to a higher standard if we are to enjoy success in the short-term and long-term. It is not enough for a person to be good at what he does; he must impact people around him in a manner that makes them better. Again, you see this play out more in sports than in any other area of life. Aptitude and talent are not enough—at least, that has been my experience in life.

---

14 John Maxwell, *My Dream Map* (Nashville: Thomas Nelson, 2009) p. 57.

CHAPTER 10

ENGAGEMENT: ARE YOU A REFLECTOR OR DEFLECTOR?

How do you deal with opposing personalities? Individuals confront situations differently and have their own strategies for accepting or deflecting blame or responsibility. Now we will examine whether a person has developed a propensity for reflecting or deflecting on situations, especially if the situation is perceived as a negative outcome.

At the core we ask ourselves to accept the truth about who we are, where we are, and what it will take for us to grow positively. Moreover, individuals must be willing to undergo growing pains in order to gain strength and overcome any adverse situation. In the end, we become better people for confronting these situations. This is the essence of being a reflector.

A deflector, on the other hand, is one who deviates from the original path or intended course in order to avoid conflict. Many people deflect responsibility; as a result, they never mature properly into the person they were destined to be. Deflection is being defensive and resistant to opportunity and change. This problem is shared by individuals and organizations alike.

In the book *Images of Organizations*, Gareth Morgan provides a comprehensive analysis of single-loop and double-loop learning in his discussion of organizations as brains. According to Morgan, single-loop learning "rests in an ability to detect and correct error in relation to a given set of operating norms." Conversely, according to Morgan, "double-loop learning depends on being able to take a 'double look' at the situation by questioning the relevance of operating norms."[15] Unfortunately, many organizations never reach double-loop learning and consequently fail to challenge established organizational practices that may be ineffective or outdated.

Now let's apply this to individuals. If one is a reflector, then he has become comfortable with the uncomfortable. What exactly does that mean? In order to grow personally, one must confront negative situations directly and develop effective solutions. The ability to develop effective strategies is a result of honesty about the cause and effect or pros and cons of the negative situation. Many people allow emotions and other factors to cloud their judgment so they never arrive at a place of true reflection.

A big part of finding a solution to a problem is realizing that you must remain objective about the situation in order to arrive at the best possible option. The prevailing view among many people is to play it safe and "deflect" responsibility or assign blame for a particular outcome. Too often, people do not fully challenge themselves and can live with knowing that they did not reach the best outcome.

ASSESS YOUR STATE OF MIND

Have you ever asked yourself, "How open was my mind today to the possibilities"?

---

15 Gareth Morgan, *Images of Organizations* (Thousand Oaks, Calif.: Sage Publications, 1997), p. 87.

_____

_____

_____

_____

_____

How long did you keep it open today? An hour? Half the day?

_____

_____

_____

_____

What actions were meaningful to you? Why were they meaningful?

_____

_____

_____

_____

We are not intentional enough in our approach to life, so it ends up getting away from us. Do not let life get away from you. At the end of the day, you should ask yourself, "Did I live every moment as if it were my last?"

THE DIARY OF ORGANIZATIONAL DYSFUNCTION

Gareth Morgan wrote, "Learning organizations have to develop skills and mind-sets that embrace environmental change as a norm."[16] If organizations are not aware of or pay little attention

16 Gareth Morgan, *Images of Organizations* (Thousand Oaks, Calif.: Sage Publications, 1997), p. 90.

to the forces taking shape in society, they leave themselves at a disadvantage. This seems like it should be common practice, but many organizations cannot see beyond their own doors and fail to account for changes in the economic, social, or political milieu.

Consequently, they do not prepare their workers or instill in them a mind-set that prepares them for the unknown. Rather than working with positive change, they work against it because they hang on to outdated, misinformed, and sometimes poisonous thought processes that keep them in a dinosaur-like state of mind. Many people in organizations are resistant to change and maintain the status-quo whether their work environment is functional or dysfunctional.

Perhaps you wonder why you are put in places at particular times, especially when it is out of your control. You wonder, *Why me? What did I do to deserve this?* It's said that the best teacher is life, so every situation cannot be rosy. We must learn through experience, but no one really wants to be put in a negative or dysfunctional environment. It recently happened to me again, and I found myself wondering, *Why me? Whom did I mistreat?* One day I found myself thinking that maybe I am here for a purpose beyond my own professional and personal growth. There are things, people, attitudes, and managerial and leadership styles I must witness firsthand in order to help others avoid the cycle of dysfunction. So I remind myself, *I am here for a reason.* And so are you.

What does *dysfunction* mean? According to *Merriam-Webster's*, *dysfunction* can be defined as being "impaired or abnormal functioning; abnormal or unhealthy interpersonal behavior or interaction within a group."[17] It is October 2009 as I write this, and we are in one of the worst economic slumps in the history of the United States. Americans are finding ways to deal with rude, cruel, heartless, and dysfunctional organizations for which they work because they must eat and provide for themselves and their family. Many organizations are able to live off of a steady diet of

---

17 http://www.merriam-webster.com/dictionary

dysfunction because they have just enough "functional" people to make sure that they survive. They cannot spend their way out of dysfunction because dysfunction is a mind-set that knows no racial, gender, or economic bounds.

There are dysfunctional people in all walks of life, but we tend not to see them until we have to work alongside or for them. Their inability to see the impact of their actions and the cumulative impact that it has on the people around them is perplexing. Some of these individuals are good people and may be our friends, but they should not be in supervisory or managerial positions because they undermine the success and eventually the longevity of the organization.

Typically, in organizations where you see high turnover in staff, very little worker input, rampant tardiness, and low morale, you usually find dysfunction. Dysfunction starts at the top of the chain of command and trickles down throughout the organization, manifesting itself in many different attitudes and behaviors. I have worked in higher education a number of years. I've worked in large school districts and charter schools and with mentoring agencies, and I've witnessed a pattern of dysfunctional behavior at all levels of these organizations. When organizations cannot pay people six-figure salaries, they need to provide a strong mission and vision that inspires and empowers employees so that they feel a sense of value and respect. For example, why would you spend a Saturday morning helping an organization? You need to feel something other than money. While financial rewards are always welcome, they will not sustain people for long.

ASSESS YOUR STATE OF MIND

Do you think the organization you work for operates in a dysfunctional manner? Why or why not?

_____

_____

_____

_____

_____

_____

List five signs of dysfunctional behaviors and attitudes in an organization.

_____

_____

_____

_____

_____

Are any of your coworkers dysfunctional in how they approach their positions? Explain.

_____

_____

_____

_____

_____

Is constructive feedback in your organization valued or devalued? Provide examples.

_____

_____

_____

_____

_____

Have you seen instances where constructive feedback has been implemented within your organization? If so, what was the result?

_____

_____

_____

_____

_____

Guiding Thought to Ponder

We must all recognize when we are unwilling to listen and learn information that contradicts what we feel, believe, or want to think. Reflection encourages us to remain open to the idea that we may be wrong in how we perceive the world or a situation. The question is whether we have the courage to admit that when the time arises, or whether we deflect our thinking. It is easy to accept something at face value because you do not have to think about it anymore. Organizations and people alike must think through problems and issues in order to address the root causes if they are to be successful in the short- and long-term.

CHAPTER 11

THE COST OF POSITIVE CHANGE AND SUCCESS

There are always costs associated with wants and needs in society. As I reflect on what it took for me to complete my doctorate in Educational administration, I must start at the beginning. There were thirteen years of public schooling (kindergarten through high school), four years of undergraduate education, three and a half years in one master's program, one year in another master's program, and six years spent getting my doctorate. Altogether that was twenty-seven and a half years: thirteen required by the state and fourteen and a half optional years. I have dedicated a significant portion of my life to learning and education, and I have no regrets whatsoever.

You must consider the short-term and long-term costs you will incur in order to reach your professional and personal goals in life. You may have to put off taking vacations, buying pricey cars, investing in real estate, and even getting married. Most of all, you will have to sacrifice time. When costs are considered this way, not many people still want the same goals they once had.

You must also consider the costs that pursuing a goal will exact on your family and friends.

In addition, you must understand the intrinsic and extrinsic payoffs if everything goes according to proper planning. Unfortunately, things do not always go as planned, so how would you handle it if your goals must be scaled back?

Have you done your homework? What is your plan?

Growing up in Philadelphia, I played many board games to occupy my time. I enjoyed Monopoly, Life, checkers, and Scrabble, and I even had my own chessboard, which I never learned how to play. (It may have helped to have a partner to play with, since computer games were not commonplace.) As I reflect on these games, I realize what they were building. They taught me to think analytically about every decision I made in order to win. I marvel at those who spend their time learning how to outmaneuver their opponents using their wit, cleverness, and ingenuity. I especially admire those who spend time mastering the games of chess and poker. While I consider myself a student of each of these games, I am only in the formative stages of learning. I appreciate the thinking, the extension of will, sacrificing of playing pieces, staying three moves ahead of your opponent, strategizing, and understanding how to make adjustments in real time.

Both checkers and chess require critical-thinking skills. In checkers you need to be quick, forward-thinking, and able to outmaneuver your opponent. The game of chess, however, requires another level of intensity and analysis. Players are rewarded for being methodical and developing strategies to anticipate their opponent's moves well in advance. Both games have one thing in common: you must weigh all possible outcomes before you make a move.

The goal of chess is to obtain through careful and calculated strategy your opponent's king. In order to do this, you must understand the strengths and weaknesses of the other pieces and how you can use them to gain an advantage over your opponent.

ASSESS YOUR STATE OF MIND

In life, many people move with little or no data or even outdated data. What is your mental approach to achieving success? On what information do you base your moves?

_____

_____

_____

_____

_____

Who is the strongest piece on the board? Who is the weakest piece? How do you position your pieces to move closer to the final conquest?

_____

_____

_____

_____

_____

Each piece on a chess board plays a unique role. Which chess piece do you identify with?

_____

_____

_____

_____

_____

Which piece do you represent in your organization?

_____

_____

_____

_____

_____

What separates the game of chess from real life?

_____

_____

_____

_____

_____

Do you approach life and work as a chess match? How so?

_____

_____

_____

_____

_____

If life is like a chess match, how do you determine which pieces to give up and at what time to give them up?

_____

_____

_____

_____

_____

Do you play any board games? What kinds of strategies must you employ to win?

_____

_____

_____

_____

_____

Are you able to make adjustments when adversity is staring right at you? Explain.

_____

_____

_____

_____

_____

Are you able to confront life from a position of power? Are you used to achieving all of your goals?

_____

_____

_____

_____

_____

Are you able to confront life from a position of weakness? Explain.

_____

_____

_____

_____

_____

Do you approach life to win or not to lose? Is there a difference between the two?

_____

_____

_____

_____

_____

_____

What is in your analytical toolbox?

_____

_____

_____

_____

_____

_____

CONCLUSION

We are all trying to accomplish our life goals. We want more money, a better job, more success in relationships with friends and family, or just peace of mind. What I have tried to do in this workbook is to take you on a journey of reflection and introspection in order to reach those goals. My goal for you is that you understand the power of the mind and learn to channel your thoughts for positive ends, which can only happen through intentional, focused reflection.

The MOVEME process is as a mental tool that shapes your thinking, making it more concrete and transformative. You must invest quality time in reflecting if you are to achieve greatness and success. The challenge is to think longer and richer and to be intentional about your thoughts before they materialize into choices and actions. In short, your thoughts have power, and the goal is to harness that power so that you eventually get to where you want to go in life.

Motivation, Openness, Vision, Exposure, Mastery, and Engagement are stepping stones for deconstructing your thinking. They give you a mirror in which to reflect as you confront conflict, complacency, and difficult choices. You must document them and learn from them if you are to grow personally, professionally, and spiritually. In essence, you must hold yourself accountable for the change you want to happen in your life. It starts with the right mind-set.

Marcal Graham, Ed.D

Where were you in your thinking before you engaged in the MOVEME process?

_____

_____

_____

_____

_____

Did you grow positively in your thinking? If so, how? If not, why?

_____

_____

_____

_____

_____

What is holding you back from becoming the thinker you want to be?

_____

_____

_____

_____

_____

Which part of the MOVEME process was especially meaningful to you?

_____

_____

_____

_____

_____

REFERENCES

Bennis, Warren. *On Becoming a Leader*. New York: Basic Books, 2009.

Byrne, Rhonda. *The Secret*. New York: Beyond Worlds, 2006.

Dyer, Wayne. *10 Secrets for Success and Inner Peace*. New York: Hay House, 2002.

Dyer, Wayne. *The Power of Intention*. New York: Hay House, 2004.

Emoto, Masaru. *The Hidden Messages in Water*. New York: Atria Books, 2001.

Graham, Marcal. *Leadership That Reaches Every Student*. New York: iUniverse, 2007.

Heifetz, Ronald & Linsky, Marty. *Leadership on the Line*. Boston: Harvard Business School Press, 2002.

Johnson, Spencer. *Who Moved My Cheese?* New York: G. P. Putnam's Sons, 2002.

Kotter, John. *Our Iceberg Is Melting*. New York: St. Martin's Press, 2006.

Kouzes, James & Posner, Barry. *The Leadership Challenge.* San Francisco: Jossey-Bass, 2002.

Maxwell, John. *My Dream Map.* Nashville, Tenn.: Thomas Nelson, 2009.

Merriam-Webster's Dictionary. http://www.merriam-webster.com/dictionary.

Miller, John. *QBQ: The Question Behind the Question.* New York: Putnam Publishing Group, 2004.

Morgan, Gareth. *Images of Organizations.* Newbury Park, Calif.: Sage Publications, 1997.

Obama, Barack. *The Audacity of Hope.* New York: Crown Publishers, 2006.

Olson, Jeff. *The Slight Edge.* Lake Dallas, Tex.: Success Books, 2005.

Rubin, Gretchen. *The Happiness Project.* New York: HarperCollins Publishers, 2009.

Senge, Peter. *The Fifth Discipline.* New York: Currency & Doubleday, 1990.

Weidner, Leo. *The Slight Edge.* Springville, Utah: Cedar Fort Inc., 2008.

Workalemahu, Bantikassegn. *A Guide to Fundamental Physics.* Addis Ababa University & Mega Publishing Enterprise, 2000.